INTRUDER

# INTRUDER

BARDIA SINAEE

ANANSI

Copyright © 2021 Bardia Sinaee

Published in Canada in 2021 and the USA in 2021 by House of Anansi Press Inc.
www.houseofanansi.com

All rights reserved. No part of this publication may be reproduced or transmitted in any form or by any means, electronic or mechanical, including photocopying, recording, or any information storage and retrieval system, without permission in writing from the publisher.

House of Anansi Press is committed to protecting our natural environment. This book is made of material from well-managed FSC®-certified forests and other controlled sources.

House of Anansi Press is a Global Certified Accessible™ (GCA by Benetech) publisher. The ebook version of this book meets stringent accessibility standards and is available to students and readers with print disabilities.

25  24  23  22  21       1  2  3  4  5

Library and Archives Canada Cataloguing in Publication

Title: Intruder / Bardia Sinaee.
Names: Sinaee, Bardia, author.
Description: Poems.
Identifiers: Canadiana (print) 20200342770 | Canadiana (ebook) 20200342800 | ISBN 9781487008710 (softcover) | ISBN 9781487008727 (EPUB) | ISBN 9781487009205 (Kindle)
Classification: LCC PS8637.I49 I58 2021 | DDC C811/.6—dc23

Book design: Alysia Shewchuk

*House of Anansi Press respectfully acknowledges that the land on which we operate is the Traditional Territory of many Nations, including the Anishinabeg, the Wendat, and the Haudenosaunee. It is also the Treaty Lands of the Mississaugas of the Credit.*

*We acknowledge for their financial support of our publishing program the Canada Council for the Arts, the Ontario Arts Council, and the Government of Canada.*

Printed and bound in Canada

*I've developed the ability*
*to revise*
*what I'm waiting for*

— Rae Armantrout

## CONTENTS

Blood Work / 1

1

Snow Day / 5
Nose Job / 6
After Schuyler / 8
Ornamental Kale / 9
Workshop / 10
Return to St. Joseph's / 11
The Deceased / 12
Christmas Cactus / 14
Band-Aid / 15
High Park / 16
Poem / 18
Harbour Song / 19
The New House / 20
Ample Habitat / 21
Intruder / 23
Shomal / 24
Barnacle Geese / 25
Aberration / 26
Although I Am Always Talking / 27
Flyover / 28
Residual / 30
Escape from Statuary / 32
The Scorpion and the Frog / 33
Twelve Storeys / 34
Transfusion / 40

2

Deposition / 43
October Idea / 44
Weed Queen / 45
Dawn of the Living / 46
Phosphorus and Nitrogen / 47
Shahrzad and the King / 48
Why We Eat Figs / 49
An Example / 50
Plain Clothes / 51
Nothing Is Forbidden / 52
The Marriage of Reason and Squalor / 53
Staycation / 54
Regarding Certain of My Poems / 55
Study of Mr. Mohan / 56
Salamander Festival / 57
Aubade / 58
The End of Men / 59
Deep Intent / 60
Song for the Song of the Hydroörganon / 61

**3**

Clearing / 65
Hypothesis / 67
Stichomancy / 68
Ziziphora / 70
Buckets / 71
Floater / 72
Scale / 74
Induction / 75
Triptych / 77
Bleeding / 79
Intensification / 80
Cadillac / 81
Panelists / 83
Ending / 85
Half-Life / 87
Ozu / 95
Poem / 97

*

Two Windows / 101

*Notes / 103*
*Acknowledgements / 105*

## BLOOD WORK

1

Out with the sun and the jade
It is the squelching armpit of August
When simply living is enough for people
Approaching each other with a put-upon look
This weather, what it does to you

Otherwise one must always look ahead
The potted cuttings abound with late growth
The park is dedicated to the missing girl
Love is for the lucky and the brave
You will experience good health

2

There's a joke about a juice box and a catheter
The nurse with all the piercings likes to tell
But all is haste and consternation
The doctors are braced for an arresting discovery
Consulting their palette of opiates
Devising new ways to invade the living organism

Now that the counts are down
Visitors are calm and deferential
You struggle to remember what they say
Grateful at least that the counts are in
The nurse applies a swab and starts to spin

3

If you have trouble keeping track of time
If you feel you're being punished
If you have trouble with basic tasks
Lifting a water glass

No one will hold it against you
It's like when you were younger
Someone is keeping an eye on you
It's getting dark and someone is driving you home

**1**

## SNOW DAY

In an early scene, a linebacker named Chad
chases our pubescent hero up a tree.
How now will he tell that freckled fawn from the bus stop
he stole her bike out of love?

Toothless are the smitten daughter's threats
to run away, toothless baby brother
still confusing P's and C's so he says "espalator."

Oh, the disordered furniture of days at home!
Windstorm, blackout, snow squall making everything
try on its ermine hat.
Children tease the breathless candle flames.
Children stage a wedding for the lampshade and the fern.

## NOSE JOB

He plays with the prayer stone. A skipping-rock,
spaceship, cold in the flat of the hand.
It calms him. I'll try to explain this.
A concrete three-storey tenement.
A few TV channels and the prayer call at dusk.
No friends but Tsubasa, Ninja Turtles.
He collects newspaper cut-outs of Jordan,
Ali Daei, Jürgen Klinsmann. The plastics man hollers
from his pushcart in the courtyard.
Two juice jugs for a white, denuded doll
with no hair or discernible features.
Uptown men get their eyebrows done,
nose jobs on a per capita scale. How European.
Basijis drive through the streets at times;
at times it's like someone's paying teenagers
to smoke. Dictates on hairstyles
are roundly ignored. Sanctions drive rations,
but he hardly notices off-brand colas.
Chocolate bars cut with paraffin wax. Trifles, really.
After all, people dance and have parties discreetly.
His sister rides the bus alone from school.
His uncle brings trinkets and photos
from Europe. The onion domes at Nevsky. Seltzer.
Powdered drinks with an astringent finish.
Metal mouth. He keeps gum in the tin,
off-brand Chiclets. He keeps cracking his knuckles,
clicking his tongue on his molars. It calms him,
believe me. His parents were communists, briefly.
His uncle, a teacher, fought the Iraqis.

They were boys, really. Played volleyball
over the trenches. Can you imagine? Shot
in the back of the knee of all places. A limp,
a comet-trail scar. It shows when he's sitting
and the little boy pokes it — how should I put this? —
so he can believe it. It's like the burgeoning
crook in his nose. A crease in the spine
of a book that sits in his palm.

## AFTER SCHUYLER

Darker sooner again and colder as
the sky went from gym-mat blue
to stone grey. I've done every
daily crossword since you left,
noting for your amusement
the more uninspired clues, for instance
twelve across on Tuesday, November 3,
a four-letter word for "flier": "bird."

Dear Gemini,
today the planets warn
your selflessness will be used
against you by a Capricorn.
Please tell me, call me out if this
is ever true. I think I shouldn't like
to be spoken to in placating tones,
only to be noticed like
a Japanese maple against
muted pines.

Still, one chill wind
and I'm back inside,
plotting my triumphant return
as well as yours,
repotting the convalescent jade so that
it might live to greet you
with the sun under curfew.

## ORNAMENTAL KALE

The neighbours don't
seem to mind it when I
eat the seed pods from their tree.
They're always out on some
retreat or tour — crumbling
monasteries of medieval lore,
alpine hot springs — craving
the sort of adventure for which I
feel the utmost admiration but
no desire. Today I ate
the ornamental kale that grows
outside the civic centre —
the kind of place you'd only go
to get a liquor licence, or say you find
a beehive in your yard, or you're
renovating and you need to know
if open risers induce vertigo.
There's a Sunday market in the parking lot,
a spiral sculpture made of shopping carts
out front, and now this kale,
whose smoky flavour
is traceable perhaps to
the nearby highway and goes
quite well with sesame seeds,
toasted walnuts, plus any lighter
vinegar you have on hand.

## WORKSHOP

"Write 'by the window /
the alley' in the middle
of the page, and build
your poem outward
from there," Damian says.
This has worked for her
and her friend Matthew,
who it turns out is also
a poet. "Everyone I meet /
seems to write poetry,"
a poet once wrote, then
wrote a novel. If everyone
saw me how I see me,
I wouldn't have to write
so many poems, sitting
all day by the window.
The alley is resplendent
with loose trash. A raccoon
with its back raised like
a dump truck is pulling
more trash from a bag,
enough trash to last
a lifetime if somehow
he could eat it all now.

# RETURN TO ST. JOSEPH'S

Approaching Parkside from
the park, I spot the cross
above the door where, seven
months ago, they took me in.
Twelve hours of shooting
skeletal pain with nothing
but a saline drip and a single
cup of water that tasted thick.
They mapped my insides out
with dyes and rays. Before
I was conveyed into a half-
million-dollar machine,
the lab tech kindly placed
a lead shield over my crotch.
Earlier, walking past triage,
she'd given me this look
like, *You howling, screw-
faced junkie, you won't
get to me.* So why
the change in disposition?
Was the morphine kicking in?
I had questions about
organ donation and who I was
supposed to call first.

## THE DECEASED

A son, a brother and a lover.

A thoughtful and engaging friend about whom nothing bad could be said.

A pragmatist, though not one given to the illusion of objectivity, nonetheless attuned to discourses regarding the spectral nature of just about everything, including gender, race and class, and how privilege and dispossession correspond to these factors.

Something of a gourmet cook.

Given on certain sunny weekends to indulge an adolescent preoccupation involving the close observation, dissection and sometimes even adornment of arachnids.

Concerned about strife in the Middle East, more as a result of distant and unverifiable ancestry than to a deep knowledge of the region's history, despite being sufficiently possessed of the latter to stump even the most obstinate conversationalists by tracing violent fundamentalism in seemingly disparate historical manifestations as a reaction to economic exploitation engendered by resource dependence.

Often alone.

Not inclined toward physical expressions of affection.

A nervous and erratic houseguest so prone to unannounced departure that he would warn the host of this possibility in the process of saying hello.

Unable to keep from crying at the sight of children eating with their hands.

## CHRISTMAS CACTUS

Feeling entitled
sometimes by boredom
sometimes pain
to feign a little
newfound wisdom,
you're forgiven for
acting somewhat

off. So what
if some houseplants
should die?
More than ever
people are coming
and going whose
kindness and attention
you live by

and will reach for
through the new year
when you're
snowed in, lonely
or need a hand
hauling the tree out
to the curb.

# BAND-AID

You pulled my hair because you care.
Suffering won't make me beautiful like the people
buying menthol chest rub at the pharmacy

or the trees that drop used band-aids everywhere
then feign death for a season.
I grind my teeth not knowing what to say to you.

I go through the bargain bin and eat what's
left in there for lunch: thorn oil for my ruptured cyst
and beauty cream for ugliness.

Does aspirin make you think of me?
I'm standing in the skincare aisle remembering
our trip to Montreal. How, laughing uncontrollably,

you opened the bathroom door on your face.
The pharmacist was taken with your bruise.
She pulled you near to ask if I had hurt you.

## HIGH PARK

You're in a quiet place between
school and unemployment, lying
down in the park with a scarf
over your face. I've brought a big,
boring book to press flowers in, though
these dandelions are awfully
juicy, don't you think? I'm not always
so chatty, but sometimes it's helpful.
We should've brought
a quilt to sit on. We should
wrestle in the grass like the other
boys and girls. Please don't let
the wine bottle roll down the hill.
At the base of the slope
is a maple leaf–shaped flower bed
a more zealous guide might describe
as a landmark, but today
it's filled with dry dirt.

Would it help if I was dark and stormy too?
It's a mild spring day with full sun.
No work to be done.
The cherry blossoms haven't
bloomed this year, so the few magnolias
suffer the full attention of a seasonal crowd.
Please keep off the bloomin' trees.
A cool gust over the pond
wakes up the brushed gold reeds.
Robins forage wearing burnt orange bibs.
It's a mild spring day, perfect for

purchasing lawn ornaments from roadside shops.
Blue jay weather vane, enchanted
porcelain frog. Mallards have
a sort of slapstick call,
don't you think? If I thought it might help,
I could be loud and defensive like
the red-winged blackbird, who puffs his chest
and switches his pea-whistle song
to a warning when we walk by his nest.

**POEM**

Though they aren't found in the region
nightingales persist
in the poetry of the Americas

ringing in the end of the world
in lofty oaks
in darkness

always darkness!

A bird that sings all day
a poet hears at night
and thinking *nightingale*
composes some didactic verse
more about himself
than what is most likely
a robin

Beware of what
what you say
says about you

In this way all poems are true
even the ugly ones

# HARBOUR SONG

The gulls eat trash and purge their throats of sand.
Dead trees ride their bellies down the valley.
A rainstorm mounts its theatrical finale
on the beach, and washes up inland
weary-winged and spent. Bundled in
a tattered flannel carapace, a man sleeps
on a bench, and passersby keep
eyeing him like he swindled them
out of something and they want it back.
The shore abuts a slope where sumac grows
in clustered beads like salmon roe.
Bottle flies spar over some rotting gore
the lake's coughed up. Daylilies loosen their bonnets.
A ferry pulls into the pier with nobody on it.

## THE NEW HOUSE

The new house down the street
is done. Men who spent
all summer on that scaffolding
dismantled it today and rolled up
their spool of orange fencing.

Crammed into a bungalow's lot, this
many-gabled and uncompromisingly
stucco affair invites comparison
to a mushroom patch. It smells like
new money and cedar planks.

Someone — the realtor — plants a sign in the lawn
bearing his own clean-cut face.
He's on the phone, leaning on his sedan,
touching base with someone vis-à-vis
the removal of the portable john.

# AMPLE HABITAT

At first I thought it was music:
the sound of a hammer dropping down
three flights of scaffolding at the former
Perth Avenue Methodist Church, a 40-unit
loft conversion so plagued by setbacks
its billowing tarps and idolatrous slogan —
"Praise the Loft" — have become
as emblematic of the neighbourhood
as the railroad bells or the briny lard smell
from the gelatin plant. At least
nobody was hurt. Hating on this city
is a rite of passage I embrace
to demonstrate my love. City of delays,
egregious detours, great rebar
obstacle courses; of mid-rises aging
without grace, like tulips.
Remember the first place we looked at,
by the corner store at Dupont and Perth?
A garish bachelor with pigeon wire
on the window ledges. They ran out
of applications so we listed our references
on a napkin. We visit friends in basements,
converted factories; small, unlikely spaces
where light must beg its way.

Public meetings have concluded for the planned
rail bridge whose announcement last spring
inspired apocalyptic lawn signs.
Local property owners were suddenly
concerned about the fate of a few

Siberian elms. We keep to ourselves
and adorn our rented strip with
porch rail planters filled with frilly marigolds.
*To mitigate confinement, broaden
your awareness of the accessible world —*
it's a new thing I'm trying. I spot a cardinal
then read about it for an hour
on my phone. Last year they nested near
the brownfield developers recently filled
with precast foundation. Both sexes have
a song like shots volleyed from a ray gun.
In courtship, males attempt to place seeds
directly into a partner's mouth.

# INTRUDER

The chickens are sold, the coops dismantled
to make way for the duplex.
The duplex is rented to students.
A lamb is killed to mark the occasion
then disposed of uneaten.

The gate is disfigured.
Its Persian inscription
resembles the vines that hem in
the lane, its cobblestones jumbled
by decades of tremors.

The armchairs, the ottoman, are paisley upholstered.
An unposted letter on the rolltop desk
tells of the latest earthquake: how, when it came,
he gathered the prized Turkish tea set
while she took down the frames.

The stained-glass transom is fractured.
Sparrows and grub worms have annexed the garden.
The gridlock, a recent development, is scoured
by peddlers who canvas stopped cars
like worker bees harvesting flowers.

A yellowing leaflet
on dealing with scorpions
sits on top of a stack on the shelf:
*place a bowl or a cake lid over it*
*and the intruder takes care of itself.*

## SHOMAL

In that place, you could dig for water
with a spoon. Mountains

overlooked the south, a sea corralled
the north. We lived there for a year.

I remember citrus trees, a roundabout
and the luxury hotel where

foreigners with bald, veiny arms
played tennis. I planted

pomegranate seeds and didn't
go to school. I found a beach stone

that looked like a fried egg
and tasted like the beach. I can't sort out

the details I remember, but like guilt
they seize me in subsiding waves.

# BARNACLE GEESE

Barnacle geese enjoy Nordic palatals,
stone-relief fish beds, and aberrant gulls.
When shellfish submerge and wash up riding buoys,
the geese fly one lap, plunge into the fjord, ease

back their black neckties and splurge.
Barnacle geese sing to their children
then push them off cliffs to see if they'll live.
No trust falls. No terrestrial birds.

Barnacle geese sing to their children
then teach them the words. We'd call this stoic:
ask Goose Dad for insects and have your pick,
but ask about sex and he'll make you eat fins.

I saw it last Christmas: Mom gutting the bird,
bailing fistfuls of pebbles and sand from its craw.
She took out its windpipe and voice box intact
and blew out a goose call all the neighbours heard.

Goose heads on platters with poppyseed loaf.
Goose born of driftwood in barnacled reeds.
Goose on the cliff with sisters and brothers.
A few on the ledge, a few in the water.

# ABERRATION

The tentative being, translucent and exhibiting adaptive boundaries,
quivers. It touches everything once. Scales form rapidly.
Hello sweetheart. This is not the travesty of early trials.

Isn't that right? Those steep incisors bear no semblance
of their design, no memory of who severed them from
the tentative being. Translucent and exhibiting adaptive boundaries,

it deserves the pleasantest stimuli: feathers, glittering fibres.
Like a dolphin, it sheds constantly and does not sleep.
Hello sweetheart. This is not the travesty of early trials.

Nourish it with oyster shells and lime, swan eggs
to modulate its pitch, to make immutable what is merely
tentative. Being translucent and exhibiting adaptive boundaries

is only natural until its personality begins to cohere,
when the first demanding groan issues from its hollow chamber.
Hello sweetheart. This is not the travesty of early trials,

this is not the oblong rug with eyes, the horned flower spraying blood,
or the strip of skin inching back toward its dish to die — only
a tentative being, translucent and exhibiting adaptive boundaries.

# ALTHOUGH I AM ALWAYS TALKING

There is an air, among
these miniature plateaus,
of childhood tucked away.
Sunlight disappears here
like cheddar into

a dog's mouth. This
is my desert island mood,
as free, surely, as I have
ever felt. I have the muted,
toothless hunger

of a worm dividing itself,
the eagerness to occupy
your disregard. Love
outside of habit
is occasional, punctuated

with fatigue,
like the weather. My million
contrary espousals,
my regimen of sleeping late,
my clear city streets, reveal

a life lived outside of any
local sense. I have conquered
vast provinces. I have
tasted every species
on the mountain.

## FLYOVER

People are in the news
for licking ice cream in the store and putting it back.
One is facing twenty years. The plane dips

like a warm spoon into the clouds
toward gridded subdivisions, in-ground pools
like marble slabs. Pedestrians

cross a wooden walkway
suspended over a large pit filled with construction beams.
My ears pop. As ever,

much of the populace
is employed in actual trades.
Then there are the "analysts"

manipulating symbols.
Lawyers and coders. I could sell a think piece
linking polyamory to housing costs.

It's hard to justify
a harsh sentence for the ice cream lickers
given the unmitigated contamination

of the future as a whole,
the hollowing out of so-called "flyover country."
I should've taken the train.

I would've been a musician
if I had more talent and less good sense.
Each month I put a little bit away.

The commentariat is divided
over the fascist movement: a looming threat
or a rock in society's shoe?

I'm not sure where I stand,
but I'm looking at the situation from a distance.
I'm making a list.

RESIDUAL

— After Michael Hofmann

Turns out we didn't have to wait till 2049.
The techno-dysfunctional afterworld's already here,
albeit somewhat unsexy. More Verhoeven
than Villeneuve, more vape lung
than vaporwave skies—granted, the pacific coast's lit up
for a third straight summer. Bummer.

Holding my civic head high, I count out
six paces on the droplet-prevention mandala
decaled on the train platform, but the hand-san dispenser's
out again (or still). While the prospect
of another wave is entirely too real, few want
a government app that maps and traces who you see.

Except me, of the fire-emoji-as-adjective demographic.
Porn-addled, content-ravenous, fluent in 1337,
AAVE (online) and Unicode 6.0, with an adaptability forged
in the pressure cooker of two recessions (and counting),
we grew up flashing each other on MSN.
We killed cable TV and precious gems.

Today my peers and I commence a Zoom meeting
with a co-sensory ritual, each of us sniffing
a cinnamon stick in our cramped rental—
ZZs and towering monsteras framing an equally cultivated,
distinctly noirish disarray—and proceed,
per the client's request, to brainstorm

search engine keywords for the nasal vestibule,
that pathogenic hotbed and untapped pharma frontier.
By week's end, a well-placed advertorial
with a punchy hed (I Decolonized My Nose,
and So Should You) will drive engagement
as the antiseptic nasal spray hits shelves.

To think our cohort was singled out
as seeking meaning over money. Any gig will do
if you can live with yourself. No doubt useful labour
takes its toll, too. My partner has nerve damage
from chiseling plaster moulds for artificial limbs.
When a biker leans too deep into a sharp

corner, or diabetes claims another leg,
or someone leaps in front of a train
and lives, numbness courses through her fingers.
At night I try to rub the feeling back in,
wondering whether this spreading out
of surplus pain is a kind of social glue or solvent—

and what is the extent of my involvement?
Is that my Bic in a dissected albatross's stomach?
What's my balance, selling words, producing waste?
Not only not knowing but balking at the question
of whether there's a purpose to this art, making a dime
and a name for myself, thinking I'm doing my part.

## ESCAPE FROM STATUARY

It's no secret some people wish they had a tail.
We're torn one by one from rolls of human Scotch tape.
Why let anger dam your heart
and turn you into stone?

Sunlight, rain is sorry.
Dark cloud, go study for the flood.
Congratulations! Your every whim brings light
to new dimensions. Even your farts are radiant blossoms

in the infrared dreamscape of the common vampire bat.
The human heart, with its plumbing
and catalogue of attachments,
branches off grotesquely in pursuit of love.

Helium, that frisky hothead
and life of every party, is running out. Why?
Maybe you ask too many questions.
Maybe it's time to let the wind have your clothes.

## THE SCORPION AND THE FROG

The ladies take their tea into the parlour.
The neighbour calls Maurice, her tabby,

in from the courtyard. The language exercises
carry on into the afternoon. When we sleep,

we must never trust a lazy dog
to guard the henhouse. Is this correct?

My, what a buttery loaf. Who can say
what the tale of the scorpion and the frog

teaches us about trust? When we dance,
when we pace with grace, we land

on the soft C. But it's that element
of risk, a sheet of air under our feet,

that makes the frog say OK.

## TWELVE STOREYS

1

The first procedure after I'm admitted to the ward is the insertion of a central venous catheter into my chest. It's a hollow silicone tube connected to a large vein above my heart. The other end diverges into two lines with dangling plastic caps like a bolo tie. If I don't tape the caps to my skin, they bounce off each other and clack like dice. This is one place chemo goes.

2

White walls, beige bed, white sheets. A mattress encased in plastic, where I spend most of the day. No get-well bouquets, no orchids, no succulents — no plants allowed. IV pumps issue alarms deep into the night. The precise word for all of it eludes me. Have my gums always been so *tight*? My nail beds so raised? Hydromorphone doesn't stop the pain; pain courses through the body and I don't feel it.

3

Each drug comes with a fact sheet photocopied so many times the text looks snowy. Doxorubicin, a compound isolated from soil-based microbes, is the colour of cranberry juice. Vincristine, derived from the periwinkle flower, makes my fingers and toes go numb, so they switch me to vinblastine, also from the periwinkle flower. The medications are prepared in the hospital pharmacy in the morning, stored in fridges and injected in the afternoon. They feel cold going into my chest.

4

M., my roommate, says they conduct animal testing in this hospital, just a few floors down. Seven years ago, in his late twenties, he was diagnosed with the same cancer I now have. We have the same doctor. He went through the same treatment. It worked, and he moved on with his life as a Jays fan. This winter, he was wiping snow off his windshield when he slipped and broke his arm. It turned out his bones were porous; the disease was back. He got the same treatment a second time, and it didn't work. Now he's receiving an experimental drug administered non-stop via a battery-operated pump he carries around in a fanny pack. It burbles like a fish tank. Every few days a nurse pricks M.'s finger to check for diabetes, which somehow is a possible side effect. He says he read online about a guy in Russia who participated in an early trial and grew scales.

5

Staff don't like the idea of in-patients walking around the hospital alone. A small roster of porters wheel me from the ward to appointments, procedures and scans. They are hurried and not talkative, always being paged to go somewhere else. I've spent hours in hallways waiting for porters to wheel me to parts of the hospital that, were it permitted, I could walk to in a few minutes. Motivational posters placed at eye level confront the wheelchair-bound with a mixture of self-empowerment and bellicosity. With great fortitude you endure and struggle, you realize and actualize, then together we fight and win. One poster just says "YES WE CANeer" above a picture of a dove. Some merciful soul has removed most of these from the leukemia ward. On the wall by my bed there's only a whiteboard with my daily blood counts. When my white blood cell count gets to zero, they'll ease the treatment to let the cells form again, then test to see if the new cells are cancerous.

6

At the end of my first week in the ward, when my hair is still all there and it doesn't yet hurt to eat, around midnight, after the other patients have gone to sleep, I see a rabbit. It pauses in the doorway without regarding me, then continues down the hall. Even if a test subject managed to escape, the nurses later explain, there are too many floors between the labs and the ward. You have to remember, in your condition, the painkillers, chemo, sleep pills, not to mention stress....What can I say? I saw what I saw.

7

By the middle of week two it takes effort to keep my eyes open. With the exception of a three-hour window once a week, the port in my chest is always connected to something. Each morning a nurse retrieves three vials of blood from it, her face close to mine. I spend the following hour willing myself into a walk around the ward, dragging the drip stand and pump as it flushes saline, chemo, blood transfusions, potassium, painkillers and other solutions into my body. The fluids go right through me. I pee into a plastic jug, note the volume, dump it, flush it, then record the measurement on a clipboard attached to the door. Nurses tally these numbers in pursuit of equilibrium. How much water did you drink today? Sometimes when the pump finishes I silence the alarm before a nurse hears it, soaking up the mute, momentary stillness, a fountain at rest.

8

M. offers me an all-dressed chip. No—my mouth has too many sores. Plus, his hand has been in the bag. They're strict about contamination here. If you have a virus, or might have a virus, you're confined to your bed and cordoned off behind a curtain. If you're sniffly or raspy, a nurse jabs an extra-long Q-tip so far into your nose it feels like they're swabbing your brain. To avoid infecting your roommates, you can't use a shared washroom and have to shit in a commode chair, which is a chair with a hole and a bag. If the swab comes back positive, you could be shitting in a chair for days, assuming the virus doesn't kill you. Which is why the nursing team is annoyed with M., who snuck out of the ward to buy all-dressed chips.

9

Tests are mostly conducted on mice, and occasionally rabbits or gerbils. Less often, on dogs and primates. Bioluminescent imaging of tumors is one example. A mouse the colour of a cloud is carried in a plastic tube—this, it is believed, is less stressful than being lifted by the tail—and deposited in a black box mounted with a low-light camera. When the box is closed, the fidgeting creature is invisible, its hindquarters ablaze on the screen.

10

Pain interrupts my thinking. Drowsiness leads me in loops. I give up on *Moby Dick*, then on *Teach Yourself Mindfulness*. My head aches all the time. If the internet works well, usually before and after the daytime hours when the outpatients downstairs are using it, I watch old sitcoms on my laptop. *Whenever I find myself growing grim about the mouth; whenever it is a damp, drizzly November in my soul*....I check my email. I apply for EI sickness benefits. Meals are either overcooked or refrigerated to the point of near-freezing because the absence of white blood cells means I have no immune system. *I bear my being without defenses.* Tuna sandwiches, inscrutable stews and steamed vegetables arrive on a tray beside a cold, unripe banana beaded with condensation. I give up on *The Big Book of Quick Crosswords.* The same people deliver and collect the trays, politely avoiding eye contact.

11

How are you feeling? How many times have you watched this *Fresh Prince* episode? Have you been able to get some writing done? Did you get my message about the study involving avocados? Have you tried turmeric? I'm assuming you're avoiding processed foods. To each their own, I guess. My old classmate had the same thing. My friend's mother-in-law. My brother's piano teacher, I think they were close. I'm sorry for the delayed response. I know you're probably tired of talking about it but I have been looking into this. I don't get it. What is there to be embarrassed about?

12

The experimental drug isn't working, M. explains. He is counting on a stem cell transplant from his brother. It involves little effort from the brother; the procedure on his end is not unlike giving blood. But before they can conduct the transplant, M. will have to be moved into quarantine and given high doses of chemo until his blood counts hit zero. Ideally, his body will accept the new stem cells and his bone marrow will start producing his brother's blood. Possibly, his brother's donated cells will attempt to fight off M.'s unfamiliar cells and destroy his body in the process. A porter has arrived to take me to the ultrasound clinic. The discovery of a small lump in one of my testicles is being managed by the doctors with practiced equanimity and alarming promptness. I tell M. to take care and I'll see him later.

**TRANSFUSION**

I walk most days before dinner
now that the air is finally calm and clear,
and each time the horizon admits more
of the visible world. The windowsills are lined

with potted herbs. A fleet of rental toilets
is converging on the park, where blue squills
bloom like dye in water. Welcome
to the party: an ache in my head I could
crawl up into, abetted by spring rot.

Curious provisional sprouts betray
the dreaded taproot, but I'll clear the yard
for pole beans and baby beets, keen
as the Sun-Maid girl, O Spring, if you
promise me more light and good, clean blood.

**2**

**DEPOSITION**

How harrowing the prospect
there may be no clandestine agency after all,
only our clamouring until we've built
something we'd sooner take up arms for

than name. By now there ought to be
some sort of saying for it:
to march all day through toppled statuary,
surprised to find oneself inclined

toward such hopefully destructive sentiments
as might find expression
in a goose-step chant.
I love my people, even you

who harbour a private vision
of the future, one that alarms even you,
that scales your fortitude
then pleads for understanding.

## OCTOBER IDEA

for J.B.

A breeze comes through the window
bearing smoky autumn odours and a wasp.
I've written about this several times already,
how the wasp traces a line around the silence in the room. . . .

I want to welcome the world, all of it,
even the guy scattering leaves with a gas-powered blower,
to believe in something
that like a giant elm presides over us

even as it diminishes.
When we were strangers at the gate,
I was the little ingrate who pissed his pants
in the airport taxi. Thankfully, those people

have been replaced piece by rotting piece
like ancient ships, their names
and old scars painted on anew
to propagate a memory of themselves.

# WEED QUEEN

We would do well to purge the language
of ambiguity. Take for example the Weed Queen.
Her business has been decimated by unhappy reviewers
whose grievances are largely traceable

to a single misunderstanding.
But to attempt this is to summon a legion of hucksters
each armed with a private truth. Signs are torn
from utility poles, exposing

more signs: Odd-Job Bob; defaced missing persons;
MY PASSION IS TO PAINT!
One curative for doubt is to tell others what to do.
You must change your hair, your lover,

your life — pare it down to only what is essential,
sparks joy, or holds vital meaning. For example,
red meat and potatoes. For example, yellow poplars
in their deep green sleep.

## DAWN OF THE LIVING

Cunning, barbaric, choleric,
with values either questionable or dangerously obscure,
they are coming here in droves, literal hordes,
to grope and/or cover up our women.

To convert and marry our children
to theirs, and muddy the proverbial waters
on a scale unseen in centuries. From all seven corners,
in the squalid holds of ships, on trains,

crossing pristine frozen plains on foot,
crowded onto makeshift rafts like scorpions on a turtle's back,
they are coming for a free bus pass,
for monthly stipends or months in jail,

restoring ancient institutions, shadow chambers,
to dictate conformity of speech and dress
till they are us, to occupy
then estrange us from ourselves.

## PHOSPHORUS AND NITROGEN

I have written elsewhere that the worm "worms."
I have made the grass grass. In the glorious first days
of the Republic, the professor of poetry
is observed buttering his bread on the balcony

while insurgents storm the halls.
It proved short-sighted in the end to tether the economy
to the exchange of stylized photographs of goods,
rather than goods themselves. In the end,

the heat-seeking missile ventured all the way to Yemen
to find what it had carried within itself all along.
Once these verses become indecipherable,
I will have achieved postmaterialist transcendence.

I shall be reassigned to the sinuous palaces of our allies.
Only then, under constant surveillance,
under lock and key, may I be free
to explore the kingdom within myself.

## SHAHRZAD AND THE KING

I have heard, O king, that the *faqih*, having been
tricked out of his robes by the wily girl,
and still possessing the saddlebag containing the gold,
left the palace before dawn and entered

the stables, intending to procure sackcloth
and an excellent horse.
Each translation is a little different.
In one, the gold is held aloft and said to gleam like a lamp.

The king can't remember if they're inside the sailor's voyage
or the gardener's didactic digression
about the great noise and difficulty of slaughtering mules;
but he would like, before being drawn back to knowing,

to linger in this interstitial moment
as one pauses in a hall with many doors,
as dawn breaks and Shahrzad trails off
from what she has been allowed to say.

## WHY WE EAT FIGS

for P.G.

Long ago, when bread ripened on the breadfruit tree
and animals spoke the language of men, there lived a widow
with three impetuous sons. Many ages ago,
when God lusted after mortals in the guise of a swan,

a sailor who was thought to have perished at sea
reappeared in his village carrying an enormous egg.
They asked him: Whence did you acquire such an enormous egg?
One day, a plowman was struck by lightning, and vanished.

His wife was sick with grief. The liver of a rabbit could not cure her.
She was not cured by the fruit of the Tree of Forgetfulness
or the song of the Enchanted Lute. The shepherd visited her.
She was visited by Wise Men, Holy Men,

even the King. Her cries became so haunting
she was locked inside a tower with a fig-shaped dome.
This is why we eat figs on the Night of the Harvest Moon,
why we open our doors on the Day of Atonement.

## AN EXAMPLE

After he captures the city of Kerman in 1794,
Agha Mohammad Khan, whose castration at a young age
should have invalidated his claim to the throne,
decides to make an example of the city's inhabitants

for sheltering the previous shah. Men are decapitated,
children blinded and women carried off into slavery.
The tyrant orders his men to gouge out the eyes of each man.
The tyrant erects a pyramid of skulls.

Forty thousand eyeballs are gathered in a pile.
Blind children wander to neighbouring villages
to tell what happened in Kerman or die of thirst.
For a meal, blind beggars throughout the empire

tell the story of Kerman's blind children.
How they must be sheltered in secret, out of sight,
for the new monarch will not tolerate opposition.
A period of relative stability begins.

## PLAIN CLOTHES

Safe now outside the committee building,
he feels no shame. Why should he?
There is no Madonna cassette stashed in his glove box,
no satellite dish on his roof. He has done nothing wrong

and told them as much, instead decrying the immodesty
of today's fashions: lipstick, loose headscarves,
men with their eyebrows done!
The youth don't remember life before the revolution,

when people dressed as they pleased, but couldn't remark
on the weather without fear of an undercover agent
dragging them off to pull out their fingernails.
When you needed to forget names, entire conversations,

lest they be pried from you in some dark chamber.
Even then, he questioned those who dressed conspicuously.
Whose attention were they seeking?
What were they trying to get him to say?

## NOTHING IS FORBIDDEN

Only the truth will stand on the other side,
and I am truth itself. I am the president's
interminable necktie, his unabridged Dickens,
the words you have been reading

and reading into. When poets say,
*The air could not reveal itself without you, lark,*
remember I am both the air
and the lark. Think of me

more faithfully and often
than you breathe. I will allow you
to stare at the sun. I will dismantle the sun
into sleep, colour and food. Your sickness,

the violence of your existence, is parenthetical
to my delight; I rewrite it as I please.
Come forth into unguarded pastures,
but not because you are free.

# THE MARRIAGE OF REASON AND SQUALOR

Some people, when they read about physics,
begin to doubt the very possibility of colour and light,
to ask if what they see is really there.
Dark as a drain, flat as a shadow, the thick concentric bands

of black enamel paint suck all the light from the room.
The painting doesn't defy interpretation
so much as consume it like a black hole,
asserting its own opacity. What you see is all there is.

Oil, glycerin, pigment, linen stretched over wood,
the letter M. If the motion of light were slowed,
we might see the artist applying his hair
to the canvas, advancing a claim to freedom

from the hegemony of figurative language,
so to speak. No God, but a curious mind perhaps
with a magnifying glass. No meaning
but the tales we tell to dispel the dark.

## STAYCATION

The locals appear happy, if somewhat remote,
emerging from walk-ups, their expressions marked
by an irrepressible self-consciousness betraying youth.
They would kill for a cup of coffee and something to eat.

Pallets have been trucked in and stacked in bulldozed lots
to feed the tower cranes that pull new property
out of thinner and thinner air.
Mid-rises with drippy window units,

a bouquet of sewage and leaf rot
that brings tears to the eyes. With time,
the most loathsome aspects of a place
become its texture. Over on the hill above the road,

an officer of her majesty's guard
is said to have escaped the rebels by riding
into dense woods. His ghost is spotted there
to this day, grooming his chestnut horse.

# REGARDING CERTAIN OF MY POEMS

Collage does not work for me. Stringing words
like bunting between homonyms and mondegreens
does not work for me.
We were warned about paradoxes, weren't we?

By the big man with the little, high voice?
And did we listen?
I'll have no one but myself to blame
when this discordant orchestra of spoons

fails to shore up the pendulous moon.
I was a young man once, with big dreams and impressive hair.
I kept a bong by the toilet and slept in a chair.
Clouds parted before me. Beauty became whatever I saw

and truth whatever I said.
I know I shouldn't dwell on memories,
but I forget so much, sometimes it feels like
that's all I ever do beside the lake, beneath the trees.

## STUDY OF MR. MOHAN

Surely you do not eat newspapers.
Some explanation exists for how many arrive
on your doorstep — delivered from London, New York, DC —
and never seem to make their way to the bin. In the laundry room,

the elevator, striding stork-like down the hall,
quiet as a bug in a mug, you sometimes
cough. You repair little Ginny's drone
when it gets caught in a willow's hair. She thanks

your widow's stare. For you are someone's Penelope,
and we would gladly have signed for deliveries
of your mother's medical shampoo till our hands turned blue.
We miss your presence at the park, Mr. Mohan,

devoted son to the bitter end. How you needed only
to be told about a blossom or some unlikely bird
to come running with your camera,
your trove of silence and your little dog.

# SALAMANDER FESTIVAL

Out here, they'll let anybody drive.
It makes no difference to the river burrowing under the road
if an out-of-towner wins the pie-eating contest.
Only that the presence, in the late afternoon's

protracted shadow, of bright clothes
and children somersaulting in the old churchyard
vindicates a sense of anticipation
carried resolutely through the first half of the year.

We were fools to think we could be happy
anywhere else. Rest assured,
someone will pay dearly for this oversight.
Others are already on their way

to take in the dense growth of birches
and how lavishly the sumac burns
throughout that charming hamlet receding in the mirror
in the sun-choked silence after rain.

**AUBADE**

He said go get your kicks somewhere else.
He said why not try *this* on for size.
A warm gust jostles the blinds and light seeps into the room.
In all of this is no measure of humility,

for it was meant to turn out this way, with a bucket of ice
and some quack from the island,
his nebula of acne scars lending the dalliance
a brutish air, with a hint too

of something remotely dangerous.
The ochre sky is dark around the edges, like a big sliced plum.
The landing planes drown out
a Chevy's phlegmy rumble

as it nears. Starved anticipation
brought them here, where the roads all lead
to water, and all the cellphone towers
go offline during a storm.

## THE END OF MEN

It is so hard for some men to be men
and be humans also, to be men without treading
on other men, as if not all men can be men.
A man needs a man like a fish needs a hook,

for how else will a man know he is man enough?
Next to some men, this man is a fly on a sill,
and this man is an island adrift in a man-made sea.
But a man without a plan is not a joke.

For instance: a man walks in on two men
and never speaks to them again.
When headlines proclaim THE END OF MEN,
this man, for one, is elated. Because man

is an impossible experiment. Because the ideal man,
who would be all things to all men —
yes-men, ladies' men, men of letters,
men of God — is a man at odds with himself.

## DEEP INTENT

I feed the algorithm everything—tasting notes for Riesling,
condo listings, *The Arabian Nights*,
the Senate intelligence committee report on torture—
to render an uncanny likeness

of our common horizon, what Pound called
"An image / Of [our] accelerated grimace."
This was before he embraced fascism,
before his sympathies got away from him,

which is also a human condition. A neural network
might mistake a photo of a titmouse for soft porn,
but it can also process every photo ever
until it learns the difference. A human could not do that.

Sisyphus could not go up and down the hill
till it was flat. So I feed the algorithm everything
from birdsong to Borges. It is my fountainhead,
my opus, my crown and crowning jewel.

# SONG FOR THE SONG OF THE HYDROÖRGANON

for A.F.

A new instrument is being built,
the largest of its kind in the world,
along the bay, where the reef once was.
You've gone about it all wrong with your soaring hymns,

with the great pipes of the organs reaching up.
Stare at the sun all you want; God dwells
under the sea. My sin is I never
learned to swim. Fearing the long, low note,

how water siphoned every word
into a pouch of air, I'd founder there
until my father fished me out.
He claims we know from birth how not to drown,

and I searched for that memory
like the crown of a sunken king, but always
came up gasping, panicked,
the sound of water draining from my ears.

**3**

## CLEARING

Mindfulness
for some

means
hosing the driveway

Stripped
of its mystical veneer

it is the disentanglement
of attention
from thought

Bindweed weaves
through a chain link fence

The prickly fruit
of a chestnut tree
smells green

Ask yourself

Do I truly own
my possessions?

Running shoes, press pot,
tree guide

Or do they

moth orchid, photograph

of Mom and Dad
at Persepolis

possess me?

With practice
a person could go hours
without thinking

The proverb about flowers
doesn't tell us
which ones are safe to eat

but we keep it
in framed embroidery
in a drawer by the bed

## HYPOTHESIS

Coconut crabs can grow
up to three feet
But did they eat Amelia Earhart?

Picture a white shore
Already there are
many obstacles

It's difficult to say what
exactly
is happening

Transmissions are heard
by a housewife
scanning her radio

Debris, light
scrawled on water
A white shore

A voice singing
*You won't be satisfied*
*until you steal my heart*

# STICHOMANCY

There is hair, yes
A fly on the sill

An itch
beneath the waxy scar

where they tapped
into a vein
above my heart

I say to the doctor
Those phlebotomists
are all pricks

My timing
is impeccable

She opens a layer
between my skin
and the air

where the spine
is ridged
like the edge of a coin

The pain on a scale
from one to ten
is seven

and rising
A sharp noise
A bed of ants

## ZIZIPHORA

Tooth of a donkey

Ashes in honey

A green bug settles
in the blue-eyed grass

*This man is fighting cancer*
*with camel piss*
*and ziziphora tea!*

But I'm not one
for magic spells
My hair is growing back

My tongue swells up
like a boat in a lock

A mute scream rises
to the surface

In chemical fog
in morning light like lunar ore

silence is my cure
and wakefulness

## BUCKETS

Like the contents
of a six-gallon "Fiesta Pail"
silver has no known purpose
in the human body

Imagine the world is dying
while you eat like a king

Jesus, on his way
to Blue Eye, Missouri,
stops for fizzy water
at the roadside Hair Museum

Oh, the wonders
people come up with
What will be remembered?

Freedom is so much
about saying no to things

Some people never
answer the door
Others hoard money

The cosmic timeline foretells
the rise of "goat nations"
Erratic rains and blight
deform the fruit

Will you be able
to filter your water?

## FLOATER

A few
harmless-seeming

weightless
blips in vision

glisten
like the trails
snails leave

Oh man, he says
that's *wild*

\*

I can't picture
myself out there

with only water
and a knife

but I'd like to see
where the blind path
leads

\*

The neighbour
strips

a blanket of ivy
from the fence

to find what?
Some sort of nest?

A blip of colour
draws

the berry pickers
and the bees

## SCALE

When one cartoon ant
says to the other

Brace yourself
for untold landscapes!

it's funny because
they're in a trash bin

Does the vastness
of the universe

make the NBA finals
pointless?

A couple of guys get into it
outside the bar

Millions of people
have watched the video

of someone crinkling
cellophane on mic

*Shrsssp*
thinks the coral

swallowing egg-shaped
plastic flecks

## INDUCTION

From deep inside the headache
I cross "mindfulness"
off the list

The day is wheeled in on a tray
between a juice box
and a cold boiled egg

Rate the pain
from one to ten

Tell me
when I touch the spot

After the night sweats stop
my fingertips go numb
and I can't face mirrors

Some of this is normal
like bleeding
from the nose

shooing away
the spiritual guides
when they come knocking

Given the results
Dad walks toward the window
and I call my boss

It's me, I'm sick

I'm sorry
who is this?

The night nurse won't say
why visitors are sobbing
in the hall

Code Blue
What am I supposed to do

That slow ghost
pushing a drip stand
down the corridor
That's me

**TRIPTYCH**

for J.E.

The hands
and wrist
in the kitchen window
slice a tomato

Is this
some sort of riddle?

You can look at something
over and over
without knowing

Open the front door
Flip to the middle
of a book

\*

The bay window
is a Bosch painting

Blood-smeared children
with feet for hands

rabbit eared, bearded
beheaded

shriek and plead

It's night
The pumpkins are alight

*

As a child
he thought grass
was called *gorgeous*

His mother would
pull up the blinds

and say, Look
it's gorgeous

**BLEEDING**

The president's bleeding
is out of control

As the second bullet
settles in his back
he shifts
in his new coil-spring bed

one of the first
of its kind

and says
I hate Mondays

Imagine the confusion
pierced by pain
Who are these men
with their bare hands

A contraption
the size of a mule

emits a sound
like thousands sighing
but fails to cool the room

Great wars
have been fought
over less than this
but not yet

## INTENSIFICATION

I want back my place
in the crowd

my old face, my job
my house in order

one table for my bread
and one for wine

In the beginning
one sickness, one language
one cure blossomed
on the same tree

There was no "I"
no kernel of me

Now I send my Kleenex
to a landfill

I take my soiled things
to the curb

## CADILLAC

It was the summer of the Denver bikini
Every other guy was wearing the same floral shirt

Pete said, Chinese doctors
are right about the tongue stuff

And it was true: people were paying $25 a month
to talk to their appliances

Meanwhile centuries of empiricism
had culminated in a revolutionary procedure

involving fecal transplants
It was the summer of the fecal transplant

I had achieved homeostasis
and was progressing to the salivary stage

when I was forced to exit the train
because a guy was wearing the same shirt as me

It was the summer the government
sunk a bunch of money into flossing

The press reported on leaked documents
pertaining to a top-clearance operation

code-named Eggburt
The prime minister tried to explain:

If you hear a crashing sound
it's probably just me in the other room

but his mouth was full of granola
which he called "the Cadillac of food"

It was the summer of whippits and ketamine
Every other guy had a Goku tattoo

but only I could ride around on a cloud
because I was pure of heart

## PANELISTS

When the panelists appear
I picture my anger
as a wall

I've been told
this is how it works

Arguing
like pissing in a pool
feels good but
is hard to justify

Like many
in my cohort
I picture the future
as a red balloon

Does this point to
a Conservative victory
or a left coalition?

The retail heiress
and the guy who coined
"enhanced interrogation"
can't seem to agree

But the numbers show
most people prefer
the colour blue

which they associate
with tranquility
and cleanliness

ENDING


Despite the crowds

despite the stench
of sweat and urine
closing in

summer at the château
is pleasant

Oh, to be gregarious
and French

A sun-baked, self-knowing
raconteur

*

Days after
the attack

the semblance of normality
resumes
its dismal reign

Did you mean *rain*?

Black hat, flight logs
no sleep

The SafePath app
would like permission
to access your location

\*

The evening seemed
to be ending on a quiet note

The samurai and the priest
sat on the church steps

having rid themselves
of the cannibals

when there came a rustling
from the woods

## HALF-LIFE

*Nothing could be worse than a return to normality.*
—Arundhati Roy

prison watchdog
in the dark

foxes reclaim
fenced off

waterfront breeze

I'm sorry for looping
videos of me
paying attention

my neighbour
was loaded
into a black van

crisp linen
cool Adirondack air

I can't breathe

when you
disinfect groceries

officer
people in driveways

can't stop
the cherry blossom

*

I haven't
worn my wristwatch
in a month

is that a deal-breaker

words of affirmation
are high in my
love language stack

my body steaming
like a cow in rain

as light breaks
down the cell
walls

wipe toward yourself
in straight
horizontal lines

looking forward
to finally gathering

strangers' droplets

a legal transaction
in those days

\*

in support of
food banks
this iconic Canadian

landlord
gets paid

hubby calls me
"little tomato"
in bed

if that means
some pensioners die

why should I

who built
a salad empire

cover your
cough

amid lockdown
clear skies

invisible to
the naked

rookie agrees
to cover tattoo

citing family
in the military

\*

Pentagon-backed
study finds

feminist boyfriend
makes me do
his dishes

banging on
pots and pans

no evidence
of bioengineering

but workers
I have eaten
everything

in a black van

peacefully
after nights of
heavy breathing

National Guardsmen
sanitize the
play area

\*

president of
counting backwards
by seven

walks back threat
to ban
"anti-boomer slur"

president of
profound carnage

bitten by emu
during quarantine

says there is
honour in it

flushing ten times
fifteen times

president of
chugging

disinfectant
UV rays

stratospheric deficit
projected

as the body
fills with light

\*

feathered pariahs
teeming on the
guano-streaked spit

before the yacht club
calls for a cull

let us grieve the future
we'd expected

peer-to-peer enabled
electric brothels
on wheels

time for a
scientific approach to

genocidaire's statue
latest victim of
online mobs

triggering calls
for military

lockdown paralysis
plagues even
the most prolific

body doubles
in the legislature

*

I had to get
a crossbow
to protect my family

who no longer
speak to me

after a plane ride
with the late
financier

and input
from allies
in the community

economist withdraws
"human wave"
scenario

in immunity
proposal

somebody has to
man the front lines

Black, Islamic
I don't care

just don't
email my wife

\*

hands in the air

I back out
of the house

credit rating
intact

after second
wave of deaths

the good news is
no other campers
are symptomatic

as tactical units
converge

looking for
viral loads
in sewers

scientists find
solitude

alters but
does not destroy
the host

# OZU

Stewed peppers on a low table: they share their precise
impressions of you

Why attend to the dream knowing it too will be written over

Your leaves are opposite, candour and austerity joined at a node

Beaming yolk of sun, the poults think the heat lamp is their
mother

The river pours itself into another, longing to be free

Which systems theory concerns the villagers sifting rubble
and ash

They should keep it brief and just chant the most moving sutras

The sky is so blue, it's sad. The actor would like tears of her own

A beloved feeds you fictions from the edge of the bed

The grain of millet stands for the young man's resilient character

Coiled snake or fan belt—splash! I make water by the road

What is it to come of age "downstream"? The free boat tours are
fully booked

So long, painted seascapes! They've replaced the word *remission*
with a bell

The question is, does it end with a wedding or a funeral

The boy is inconsolable: there will be no trip to the car wash

Such outsized moments rise to the surface like Brazil nuts

Balancing a tea tray: the middle child is born as night falls

# POEM

Three identical cars
at a crossing
Coincidence

or glitch in the code?
Why during the holidays
do people bring things

catkins, fir trees
into the house to die?
The trick

with pomegranates
is to bring them
to your ear

With red beads
dripping from his head
the king

staggers offstage
A ghost needs
vengeance

like a dog needs love
and ear medicine
A poem needs

to ask big questions
Why am I bleeding
When have I been here before

*

# TWO WINDOWS

At some point between nine and one
the pharmacy will deliver a package labelled CYTOTOXIC
which I have been instructed to keep in the fridge
until the nurse arrives at some point between one and five
to inject it into my bloodstream.

All day, the patient anticipates an interruption
whose perpetual imminence constrains the poet.
As luck would have it, it's the perfect day to be outside.
Sunlight stretches over mid-rises to the southeast.
Someone has cleared the ivy and rotting crab apples from the corner lot.

A quarrel of sparrows animates the mulberry.
They go quiet when people pass by, which makes them invisible.
They don't mind the crossing guard who rises occasionally
to produce an orange whistle from one of her innumerable pockets.

The first bell from the school up the street
and the churning and hammering at the townhome development
are drowned out as a freight train thunders through the station
at five times the speed of the airport express.

The neighbour lets her Yorkshire terrier out to pee by the back shed.
She sweeps the narrow alley between our houses
then she sprays the ground with a hose.

There goes the late bell for the tardy kids.
By now the sun must be halfway over the rooftops,
shimmering with that egg wash gloss
the mind applies to what it trusts is there.

# NOTES

The epigraph for this book comes from "Results" by Rae Armantrout (*Versed*, Wesleyan University Press, 2009).

The lines quoted in the middle of "Workshop" are taken from "Better Living Through Chemistry" by Daniel Jones (*The Brave Never Write Poetry*, Coach House Books, 2011). (Thank you Damian for that prompt.)

Part 10 of "Twelve Storeys" quotes the opening page of *Moby Dick*, which I still haven't read.

"An Example" is informed by accounts of the sack of Kerman described in Abbas Amanat's *Iran: A Modern History* (Yale University Press, 2017) and *Shah of Shahs* by Ryszard Kapuściński (Vintage, 1992).

"The Marriage of Reason and Squalor" is inspired by Frank Stella's 1959 painting *The Marriage of Reason and Squalor, II* (Museum of Modern Art, New York).

"Song for the Song of the Hydroörganon" is inspired by André Forget's story "The Lower Registers."

The first sentence of "Hypothesis" is a variation on a Tweet by the Austin *Statesman* promoting a story that has since been removed from their website.

The third section of "Triptych" is inspired by Jesse Eckerlin.

The epigraph for "Half-Life" comes from Arundhati Roy's essay "The Pandemic Is a Portal" (the *Financial Times*, April 3, 2020).

In "Ozu," the lines "They should keep it brief and just chant the most moving sutras" and "The sky is so blue, it's sad" are taken from dialogue in Yasujirō Ozu's films *Late Autumn* (1960) and *Floating Weeds* (1959), respectively.

## ACKNOWLEDGEMENTS

Some of these poems first appeared in the following publications: *30 Under 30, Another Dysfunctional Cancer Poem Anthology, Best Canadian Poetry 2015, Best Canadian Poetry 2018, Best of the Best Canadian Poetry, The Best of Walrus Poetry, Arc, The Capilano Review, The Fiddlehead, The Humber Literary Review, Lemon Hound, Literary Review of Canada, Maisonneuve, The Malahat Review, PRISM international, The Puritan, The Rusty Toque,* and *The Walrus*.

For financial support, thank you to the Toronto Arts Council and the Ontario Arts Council's Writers' Reserve.

For guidance and encouragement, thank you Michael Dennis, David O'Meara, Karen Solie, and Rob Winger. Thank you to my editor, Kevin Connolly, for his friendship, book loans, insight and splitting of hairs. Thanks to the folks at Anansi — especially Gil Adamson, Maria Golikova, Jamin Mike, Cindy Ma, and Alysia Shewchuk — for their enthusiasm and attention to detail, and for preparing a bowl of M&Ms with the green ones removed.

Love and gratitude to Cameron Anstee, Jeff Blackman, Michelle Brown, Laura Clarke, Vincent Colistro, Kayla Czaga, Claire Freeman-Fawcett, Pete Gibbon, Jeremy Hanson-Finger, Ben Ladouceur, Justin Million, Hajer Mirwali, Ted Nolan, Oubah Osman, Michael Prior, Phoebe Wang, Catriona Wright, and everyone else who provided feedback. Thank you Guelph-Humber friends and everyone in the In/Words extended universe.

To the staff and volunteers at Princess Margaret Cancer Centre, St. Joseph's Health Centre, the University Health Network, and to healthcare workers at large: you have my undying gratitude.

Thank you Mom, Dad, Saba and Adrian. Kaitlin, thank you for each day.

Bardia Sinaee was born in Tehran, Iran, and currently lives in Toronto. He is the author of the chapbooks *Blue Night Express* and *Salamander Festival*. His poems have appeared in magazines across Canada and in several editions of *Best Canadian Poetry*. He holds an MFA from the University of Guelph, where he was nominated for the Governor General's Gold Medal. This is his first book.